BRITISH FIREAR[M

The Lee Enfield Number 4 Rifles

Alan M. Petrillo

Excalibur Publications

Dedication

For Mary, who always believed in me.

By the same author from Excalibur Publications:
British Service Rifles and Carbines 1888-1900
Cartridge Carbines of the British Army
The Lee Enfield Number 1 Rifles
The Number 5 Jungle Carbine

Excalibur Publications

PO Box 35369, Tucson, AZ 85740-5369
voice: (520) 575-9057
fax: (520) 575-9068
email: apetrillo@excaliburpubs.com

ISBN 1-880677-00-8
Sixth printing — February, 2001

Table of Contents

Introduction 5

General History 7

Number 4 Mark 1 13

Number 4 Mark 1* 25

Number 4 Mark 2 35

Number 4 Mark 1/2 39

Number 4 Mark 1/3 41

Number 4 Mark 1 (T) 43

Sniper Rifle Instructions 49

Sniper Sling Instructions 54

Bayonets 60

Introduction

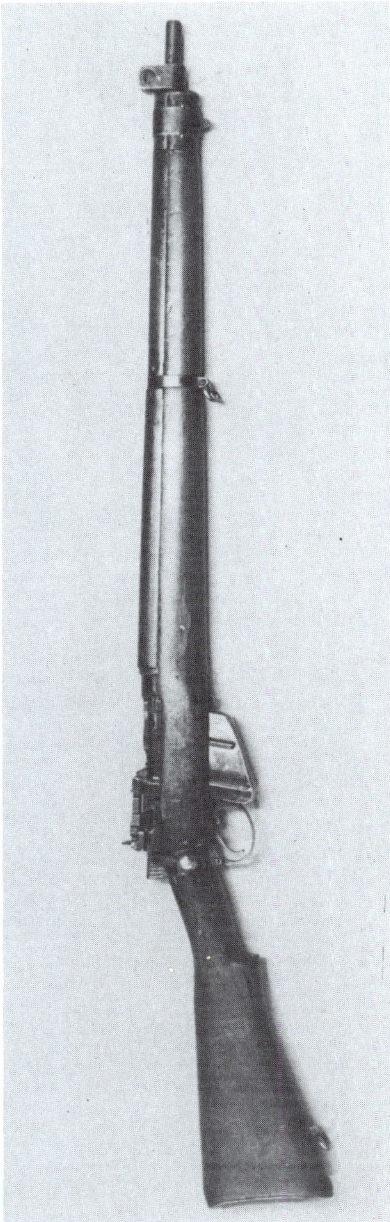

The Number 4 series rifles took the British soldier from World War II to the introduction of the L1Al self-loader.

This book tells the story of one part of a family of rifles — the Number 4 series of the Lee Enfield — which saw Great Britain through the Second World War, the Korean War, and several other regional conflicts.

Born in the 1930s from the design of its predecessor, the Number 1 Mark VI rifle, the Number 4 rifle proved to be the world's fastest operating military turnbolt rifle of its time. Indeed, there are few current turnbolt rifles of any kind which can compare with the speed and ease of manipulation of the Number 4 rifle's bolt, even today.

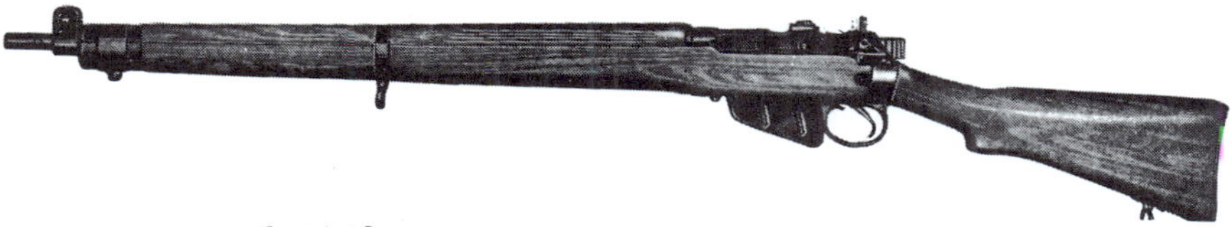

General History

The Number 4 rifle came into being in 1931, with approximately 500 test rifles being made available to the Small Arms School, the 3rd Carabineers, and the 2nd Battalion of the West Yorkshire Regiment. After several months of trials, the general conclusion was that there were a number of advantages over the then-current service rifle (the Number 1 Mark III*). These included greater handiness, better accuracy due to the heavier barrel, and improved shooting because of the aperture rearsight. At the same time, a small number of deficiencies were noted, and suggestions made to deal with them.

The next year, 1932, saw additional trials in Egypt, Eastern and Northern Commands, and Aldershot. These were followed by trials in India and at the School of Musketry at Hythe. After all was said and done, the official approval for manufacture of the Number 4 Mark 1 rifle was granted on 15 November 1939.

The Royal Small Arms Factory, at the time located in Enfield Lock, Middlesex, was the home of Lee Enfield rifles, and it was there that the trials Number 4 rifles were built. But after World War II broke out, RSAF Enfield was swamped with orders for firearms to be built, so production of Number 4 rifles was allocated to three factories.

The first British factory to make Number 4 Mark 1 rifles was the government factory at Maltby, near Sheffield in Yorkshire. Production figures show that 25 Number 4 Mark 1 rifles were produced in June of 1941 at Maltby, essentially the first official production run

Number 4 Rifle Statistics

Model	Adoption Date	Changes in Pattern
No.4 Mk1	15 November 1939	• Stronger receiver (flat-sided) • Heavier barrel
No.4 Mk1*	15 June 1941	• Bolt removal through slot in boltway •Mk 2 rearsight
No.4 Mk2	31 March 1949	• Trigger hinged on action body instead of trigger guard
No.4 Mk1/2	31 March 1949	• Mk 1 converted to Mk 2 pattern
No.4 Mk1/3	31 March 1949	• Mk 1* converted to Mk 2 pattern
No.4 Mk1(T)	12 February 1942	• No.32 telescopic sight with special mount • Wooden cheekrest • Revolving guard screw swivel • Altered Mk1 rearsight

of this family of rifles to come off the manufacturing lines. Eventually, the Maltby factory would make a total of 737,000 Number 4 Mark 1 rifles by the end of the war in 1945.

The second factory to begin production of the Number 4 Mark 1 rifle was the government factory at Fazakerley. This factory was only one month behind the Maltby facility in turning out finished Number 4 Mark 1 rifles, making its first shipment of 300 rifles in July of 1941. Ultimately, Fazakerley produced nearly 620,000 Number 4 Mark 1 rifles by 1945.

Fazakerley also was the only government factory to continue production well after the war, although one of its chief functions was to upgrade and refurbish various marks of Number 4 rifles in the post-war years.

The third factory was the Birmingham Small Arms Company complex at Shirley, near Birmingham. Production of Number 4 Mark 1 rifles began there in 1941, with the first 300 rifles turned out there in August of that year. By the end of the war, in 1945, the BSA Shirley factory had shipped 665,000 Number 4 Mark 1 rifles.

Number 4 Ordnance Marks

Six different ordnance marks were used on Number 4 rifles built during the Second World War. From left, Canadian Department of National Defense mark; mark put on rifles made at Long Branch, Ontario, Canada; flaming bomb mark of US War Dept; British War Office property mark; Stevens Arms Company trademark (second right and far right).

Thousands of miles to the west, arrangements for production facilities to manufacture Number 4 rifles were being made in the United States and Canada. In the United States, the British government first contracted with Savage Arms Company in 1941 to supply US-manufactured Number 4 Mark 1 rifles made to British specifications. The Savage firm completed a substantial portion of that contract before the introduction of a modified version of the firearm, the Number 4 Mark 1* rifle.

Since the new Mark 1* made several concessions to ease the manufacturing processes, the balance of the contract was filled with Mark 1* rifles. Production at the Savage factory was 1,325 rifles in 1941, but total production swelled to over 1.2 million rifles by 1944. Number 4 Mark 1* rifles made at the Savage factory can be identified by the letter "C" in the serial number (for example, 12C1234).

In Canada, the British government worked with the Canadian government to set up a factory dedicated solely to the production of Number 4 rifles. It was at Long Branch, near Toronto, in 1941, that the Number 4 Mark 1* rifles were manufactured. The factory produced over 910,000 of these rifles, plus nearly 1,000 sniper equipments. All Number 4 Mark 1* rifles from this factory were marked "Long Branch" on the left side of the action. Number 4 Mark 1* rifles made at Long Branch can be identified by the letter "L" in the serial number (for example, 23L4321).

Various shortages during the Second World War, as well as the need to make more and more rifles, in less and less time, led to several manufacturing changes in Number 4 rifles.

One of the chief changes one might notice is that the Number 4 series of rifles had its metal parts either browned or oil blacked. This latter procedure was a system much like parkerizing, but leaving a smooth lustre which looked like a painted finish. Fortunately, it wore much better than paint. Gone were the days of rust blue finishes from before the First World War.

Once Number 4 rifles began rolling off the production lines, a shortage of seasoned walnut developed. This shortage meant that kiln-dried walnut, as well as beech and birch, began to be used in stocking up Number 4 rifles.

Early Number 4 rifles had a majority of their metal parts made out of milled metal — bands, trigger guards, and foresight protectors among them. But again, the ebb and flow of wartime production caused shortcuts to be used. Metal stampings were used from about 1942 onwards, and proved to be an enormous benefit in saving both time and money.

Thus, four different versions of rearsights appeared on Number 4 rifles during World War II, three different trigger guards, two foresight protectors, two foresight blocks, two bolt bodies, two cocking pieces, and

Number 4 Magazine Parts

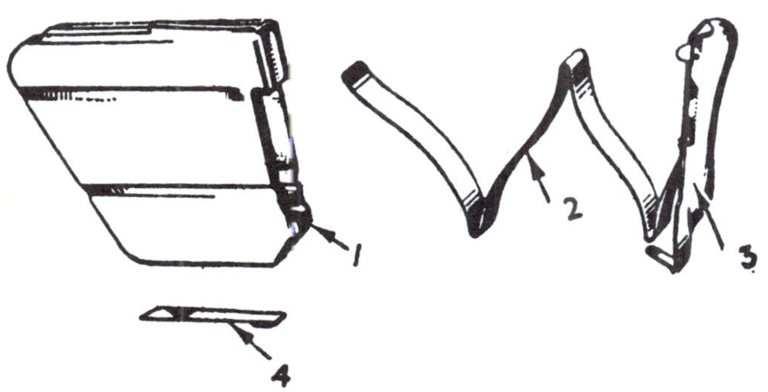

Parts of the magazine for the Number 4 Mark 1 rifle: 1. case; 2. magazine spring; 3. platform (follower); 4. auxiliary spring.

three buttplates, among other items. Interchangeability of parts was a keystone in the Number 4 manufacturing process, and the different versions of each part fit equally well.

One of the most noticeable modifications to the Number 4 rifle was the approval of the Mark II barrel. The standard barrel for the Number 4 series rifle was a 25-inch long, 2 pound 8.5 ounce barrel, with 5 lands and grooves, one turn in 10 inches, left hand twist. In May, 1941, tests were made with barrels manufactured with only two lands and grooves, rather than the standard five. After extensive accuracy and erosion testing, it was found that the two-groove barrel performed as well as the standard five-groove version.

Thus, to further ease production facilities at Savage and Long Branch, the Mark II barrel, as the two-groove version was called, was approved for use with the Number 4 Mk1* rifle.

A Number 4 rifle magazine made by Stevens Arms Company in the United States, right, is a duplicate of that manufactured by a British contractor, left. One of the prime features of the Number 4 series of rifles was the interchangeability of parts.

Number 4 Mark 1

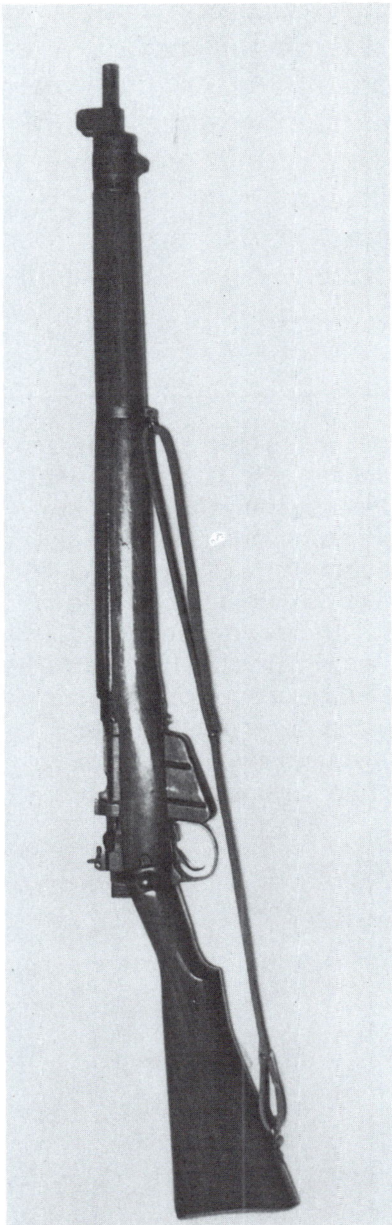

The Number 4 Mark 1 rifle was officially adopted in 1939.

The Number 4 service rifle was a product improved Lee Enfield, designed to take advantage of contemporary manufacturing processes. As such, it was quite different from its predecessor rifles, the Number 1 series.

Adopted 15 November 1939, the Number 4 Mark 1 rifle was quite literally descended from the Number 1 Mark VI rifle produced in the mid-1920s, but with a number of major modifications.

The Number 4 Mark 1 rifle featured a stronger action than any of its predecessors, with the action being easier to manufacture due to its flat sides. Those same flat sides allowed for a greater thickness of metal, without making the rifle overly cumbersome, thus increasing the strength of the rifle.

The charger bridge on the Number 4 was changed from earlier rifles, being made of two pieces, instead of a single large bridge. The contours of the charger bridge were scaled back, with the effect being trimmer and less bulky in appearance.

The receiver also features a considerably larger ejector screw, compared to those of the Number 1 series, in order to provide positive ejection with the new flat-sided action.

Another major difference from the Number 1 series of rifles can be found in the shape and design of the bolt head. Still removable, as was its predecessor, the new bolt head was of a slimmer style, with excess metal trimmed away. And as a boon to armourers, the new bolt head came in four different sizes—0, 1, 2 and 3—

Change in Bolts and Boltheads

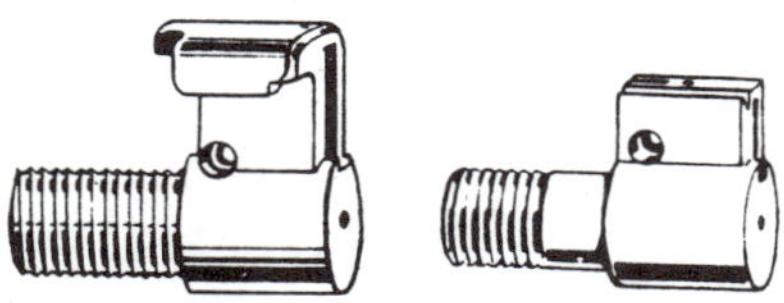

The bolt and bolthead of the Number 4 rifle (left illustration), shows a striking difference in profile to its predecessor on the Number 1 rifle. The Number 4 bolthead is on the right. Below, the complete Number 4 bolt is shown both assembled, and with the bolthead removed. The Number 4 was originally furnished with a "0" size bolthead, but four sizes were available.

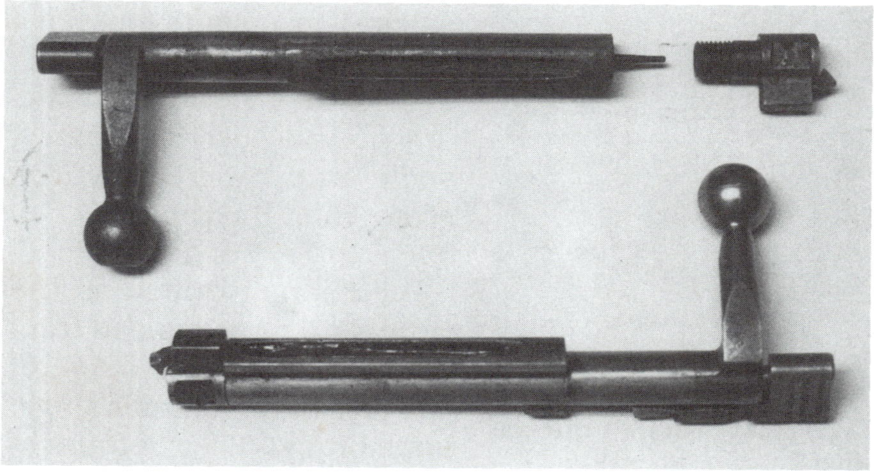

stamped on the top of the bolt head. A zero-designated bolt head was the shortest in length, while the 3 bolt head was the longest.

A longer sight radius of 28.5 inches, compared to the Number 1 rifle's sight radius of 19.5 inches, provided the Number 4 with the potential for greater accuracy in shot placement.

And it is the rearsight of the Number 4 rifle which was a great departure from previous models. The new aperture rearsight was a milled model, adjustable for elevation through a screw wheel at the top of the sight, and was graduated from 200 to 1,300 yards. The sight was hinged at the rear of the receiver, on a cross-pin engaging two small projection ears.

When folded forward, the rearsight fit into a recess in the top of the receiver. A battle aperture, sighted for 300 yards with bayonet fixed, was the chief means of sighting when the rearsight was folded forward. For ranges beyond 300 yards, the sight was raised, and was locked in place by a spring and plunger.

Students of the Number 4 rifle will note that there are four different marks of rearsights, Marks 1 through 4, produced by the British government or its contractors. The Canadian arsenal at Long Branch produced three models, while the Savage Arms Company in the United States made two models of rearsight for the Number 4 rifle.

The British, Canadian and Savage-made Mark 1 micrometer rearsights were alike in all respects, save the markings on them to indicate the particular manufacturer. All were adjustable in whole minutes for elevation through a screw mechanism controlled by a small wheel on the top of the sight.

The Mark 1 sight was graduated to 1,300 yards, had a one-half minute aperture, and needed to be raised from its recess in the

Number 4 Rearsight Assemblies
Marks 1 and 2

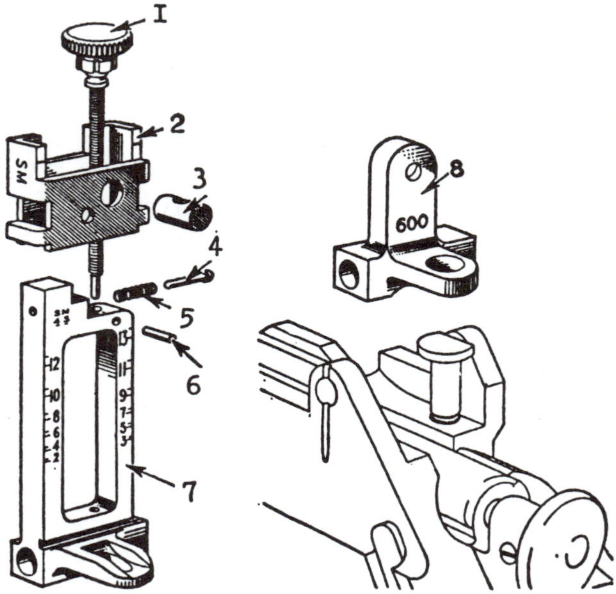

The Mark 1 rearsight for the Number 4 rifle is commonly called the "micrometer" rearsight because of its click adjustments. Parts of the Mark 1 rearsight are:

1. Adjusting screw
2. Slide
3. Adjusting screw nut
4. Adjusting screw plunger
5. Spring
6. Pin
7. Leaf

The Mark 2 rearsight, (#8), is often found on many Number 4 Mark 1* rifles made by the Canadian Long Branch factory and Savage Arms Co. in the USA.

The illustration at the lower right shows the detent and plunger mechanism for the Number 4 rifle series.

Number 4 Rearsight Assemblies
Marks 3 and 4

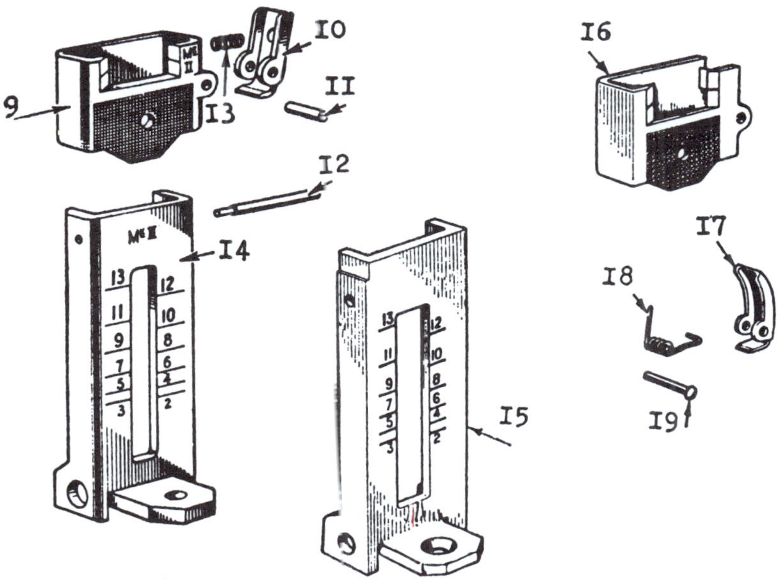

The Mark 3 and Mark 4 rearsights are sometimes confused due to the nomenclature stamped on some of their parts. For example, the Mark 3 rearsight uses the Mark II slide, which is stamped into the metal of the unit. Thus, the confusion.

Parts of the Mark 3 rearsight are:

9. Mark II slide
10. Mark 1 catch
11. Catch pin
12. Stop pin
13. Mark 1 spring
14. Mark II leaf

Mark 4 parts are:

15. Mark III leaf
16. Mark III slide
17. Mark II catch
18. Mark II spring
19. Pin

top of the receiver in order to use the scale. However, the unit also had an aperture battle sight, which was sighted for 300 yards with the bayonet fixed. The battle sight could be used when the sight was folded forward into the recess in the receiver.

The Mark 2 rearsights made in all three countries also were identical except for markings. The Mark 2 is the L-flip sight consisting of a two-position aperture sight, set for 300 and 600 yards. A simple 90 degree rotation by hand changed the sight setting.

The Mark 3 rearsight was made by all three makers, and was a sheet metal pressing of the Mark 1 sight. The unit was not as wide as the Mark 1 at the base, necessitating the use of a small collar to properly center the sight. Activation of the aperture slide was by a spring and lever protruding from the right side of the sight.

The Mark 4 rearsight was made by both British and Canadian manufacturers, and was an improved version of the Mark 3. It looked very similary toe the Mark 3, but had a full width base

The four versions of the Number 4 rearsight, from left, Mark 1 (micrometer), Mark 2 (L-flip), Mark 3 and Mark 4.

The Business End of the Number 4 Rifle

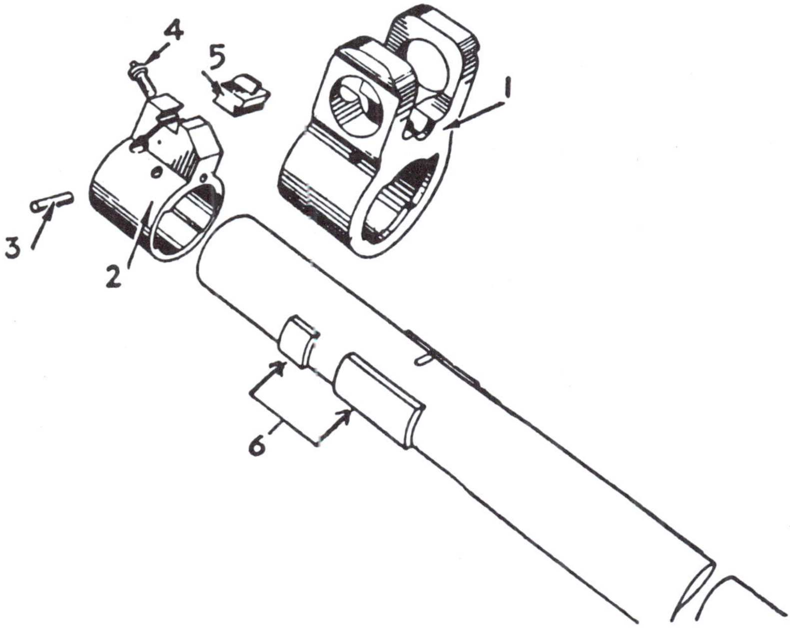

The muzzle end of the Number 4 rifle was quite different from the earlier British service rifle, the Number 1 Mark III*, in that three inches of the barrel was exposed from the wood furniture. This allowed a new bayonet to be attached to lugs cut onto the barrel, which also had lugs for the front sight block.

Parts of the muzzle assembly are:

1. Foresight protector, Mark 1
2. Block, Mark 1
3. Block pin
4. Foresight locking screw
5. Foresight blade
6. Barrel lugs
   front: bayonet
   rear: sight block

Foresight Protectors

The Number 4 had two types of foresight protector, designated the Mark 1 and Mark 2. The Mark 1 was milled of steel stock, and held in place with a threaded cross pin. The Mark 2 was designed to be easier to manufacture, and was a pressed steel unit. The Mark 2 is often found on Number 4 Mark 1* rifles. Above, a side view of the Mark 1, left, and the Mark 2 foresight protectors. In the photo below, the Mark 1 is on the left.

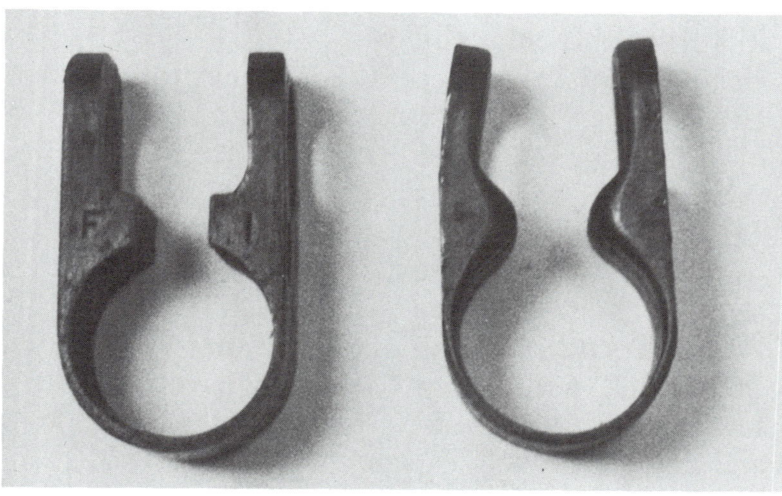

Foresight Blades

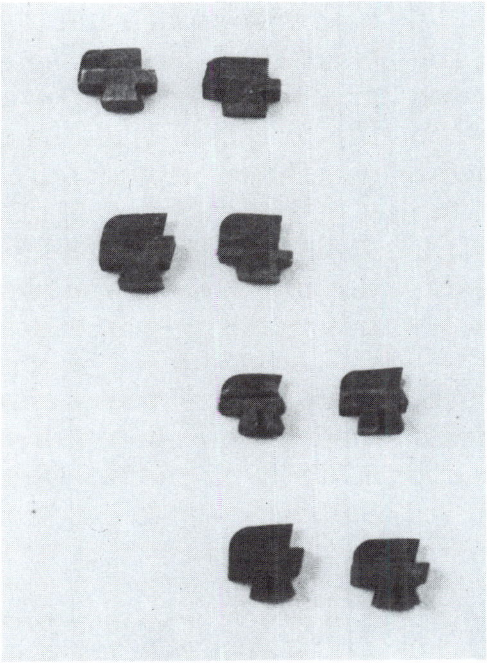

Foresight blades for the Number 4 rifle were manufactured in nine heights, and four marks. The Mark 1 was the initial type supplied on rifles, with a solid base and full blade.

The Mark 1* kept the full blade, but featured a split base.

The Mark II returned to the solid base, but had a shorter blade, measured on the longitudinal axis.

The Mark III had both the shorter blade and the split base.

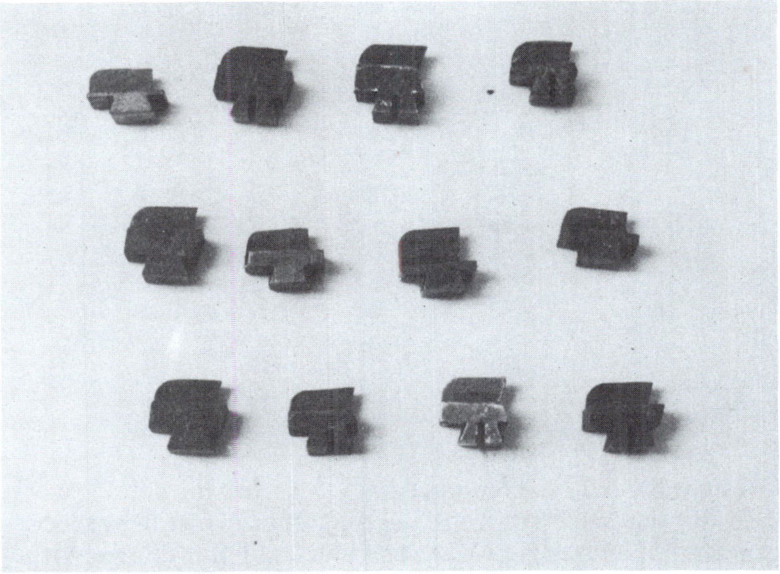

and an updated aperture slide locking spring and lever.

The front sight on the Number 4 Mark 1 rifle was a blade configuration, much like that on the Number 1 Mark III rifle. However, the blade on the Number 4 Mark 1 was available in nine different heights.

It was secured into a dovetailed block, which itself was pinned over two lugs cut onto the barrel.

The foresight block on the rifle generally is found in two configurations — one type with a split frame tightened by a locking screw, and the other which held the foresight blade in the dovetail by friction only.

The foresight protector on the rifle also was made in two models — a milled version and one of stamped steel. Most of the stamped models were made either in Canada or in the United States.

The foresight block of the Number 4 at left shows the set screw with a reverse slot that necessitated the use of a special foresight screw tool to release the foresight blade. The block at left is shown without its blade for comparison to the unit on the right.

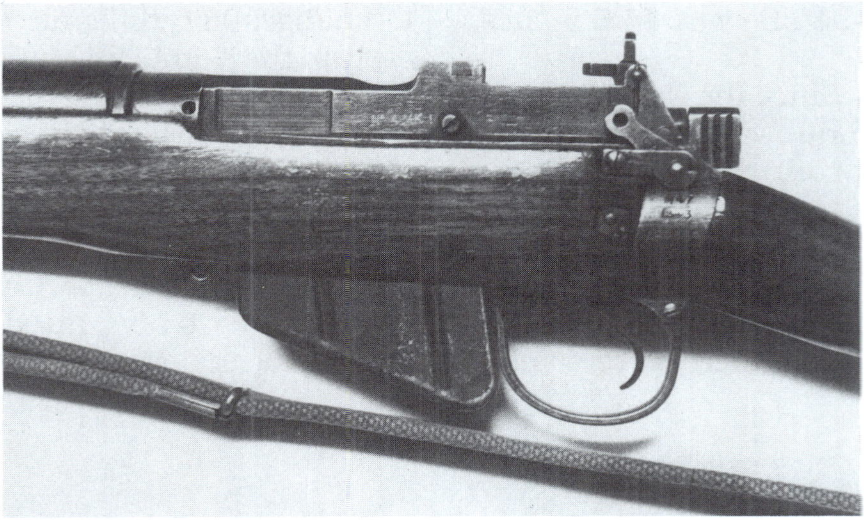

The Number 4 Mark 1 action in close detail. Note the model designation on the left side of the receiver, as well as the arsenal's stamped designation on the left socket. In this instance, the M47 stamp denotes the BSA Factory at Shirley. This rifle is fitted with the Mark 2 rearsight and the standard web sling.

Both foresight protector versions were secured to the foresight block by a small cross-screw.

The heavier barrel on the Number 4 Mark 1rifle provided greater stability and finer accuracy at longer ranges. The muzzle end of the barrel was slightly thicker when compared to that of the Number 1 rifle, and two lugs were provided on the new barrel to attach a newly-designed spike bayonet. Unfortunately, the spike bayonet, which went through several modifications, never received the enthusiastic support of the troops that the Number 4 Mark 1 rifle did.

Rifling on the Number 4 Mark 1 barrel was five grooves of concentric form, making one turn in 10 inches, left hand twist. Width of the rifling grooves was .0936 inches, while depth was .005 inch.

Overall weight of the Number 4 Mark 1 rifle was 9 lbs. 1 oz. without bayonet, and 9 lbs. 8 oz. with bayonet. Overall length of the rifle was 44.5 inches.

Since the Number 4 Mark 1 rifle was designed for mass production, all screw threads were cut to standard specifications, meaning there was interchangeability of parts between rifles. While there were some interchangeability difficulties early in the Number 4 Mark 1 rifle's manufacturing history, particularly on rifles made at the BSA factory at Shirley, these problems were soon sorted out and the various pieces of the rifle made truly interchangeable.

Number 4 Mark 1*

Just as the Number 4 Mark 1 rifle was a vast improvement over the Number 1 series of Lee Enfields in terms of production techniques, so too was the Number 4 Mark 1* model. The "*" in the designation denoted modifications to the weapon, yet none of such magnitude that the model demanded the next mark designation. Incidentally, the asterisk is generally pronounced as "star" in denoting the name of the rifle, as in "Number four mark one-star rifle."

So while the Number 4 Mark 1 was designed with the latest manufacturing process in mind at the time, further expedients were soon developed which took the form of the Number 4

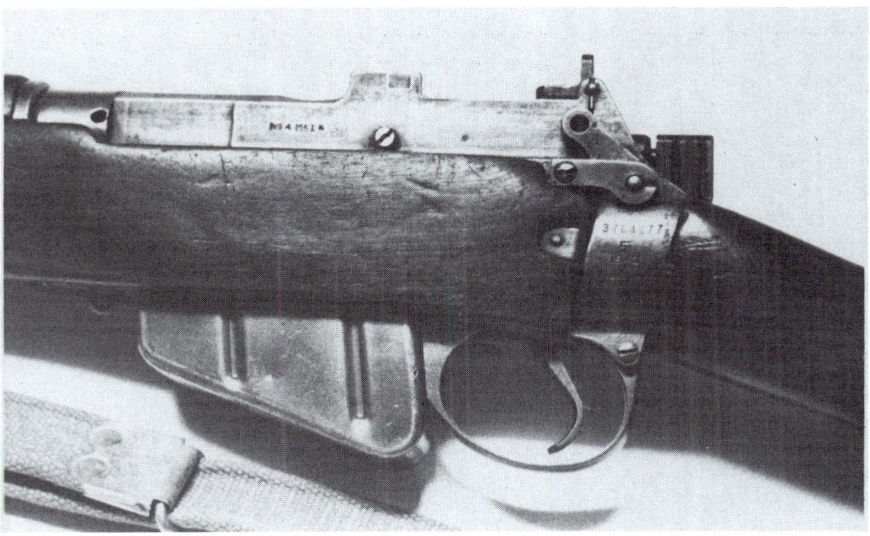

This Savage-manufactured Number 4 Mark 1* rifle was produced in 1943, as can be seen on the left socket. Along with the date, the socket carries the serial number and the Savage (Stevens) trademark "square S." The model designation is stamped on the left side of the body itself. This rifle is fitted with the Mark 2 (L-flip) rearsight.

A Change in Rifle Bodies for the Number 4 Series

Mark 1 Body

As fitted to the
Number 4 Mark 1 Rifle

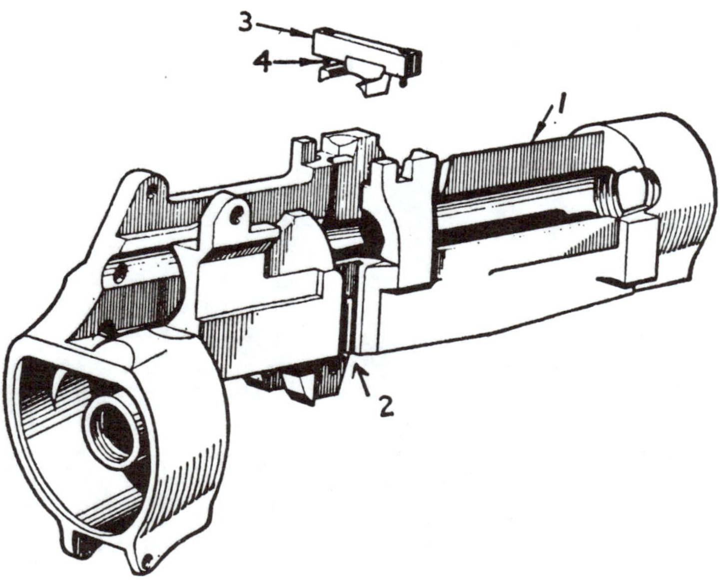

Mark 1 Body:

1. Body
2. Machining for the bolt head catch
3. Mark 1 Bridge
4. Bridge Screw

How the Body of the Mark 1 Rifle Differs from that of the Mark 1*

Mark II Body

As Fitted to the Number 4 Mark 1* Rifle

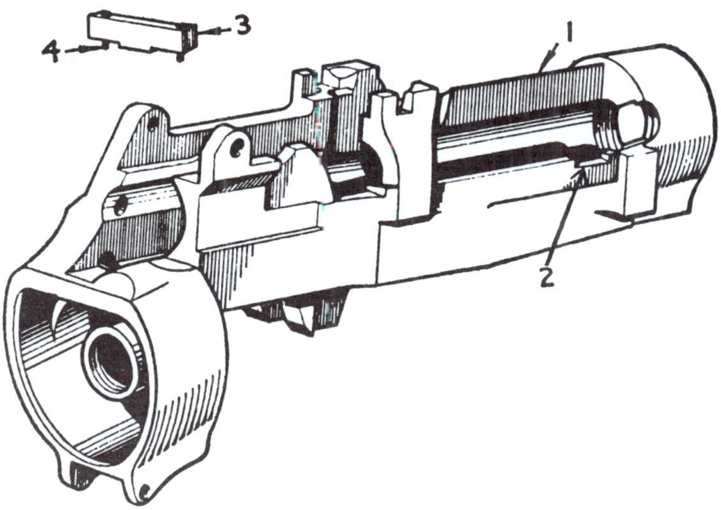

Mark 2 Body:

1. Body
2. Slot in ribway
3. Mark II Bridge
4. Bridge Screw

Furniture for the Number 4

Wood furniture for the Number 4 series of rifles consists of four major pieces: from left, buttstock, forend, top and lower handguards.

The government began the Number 4 series by putting all walnut furniture on the rifles, but demand for the weapons soon out-stripped the supply of available walnut.

In its place, the British substituted wood furniture of beech and birch. Both these woods are lighter in color than walnut, the birch much more so. Number 4 rifles with birch wood can be readily identified by their yellow stocks.

Many of the later Lee Enfield Number 4 rifles chambered in the 7.62mm NATO calibre were fitted with birch furniture.

Mark 1* rifle, adopted 15 June 1941. These changes had several noticeable features.

First was the method of removal of the bolt. The Number 4 Mark 1 rifle had a spring loaded bolt catch at the right rear of the boltway, which had to be depressed in order to run the bolt head over it and swing it up and to the left for removal. The Number 4 Mark 1* rifle did away entirely with the bolt catch and spring, and the necessity of cutting a vertical slot for them in the receiver.

Instead, the Number 4 Mark 1* had a slot cut in the bolt guide groove, about one-half inch back from the receiver ring. By withdrawing the bolt so that the bolt head lined up with the cutout, the bolt head could be raised and the entire bolt assembly removed from the rifle. This procedure saved a considerable amount of time and money in machining operations, and simplified the rifle's design.

The original rearsight on

The Safety Assembly

The safety assembly of the Number 4 series is made up of four individual pieces: from top, the safety lever, (known to the British as the locking bolt lever), and the safety catch itself, (threaded on the top of the lever; the safety screw; and the safety spring. During the production years, several types of safety levers were made.

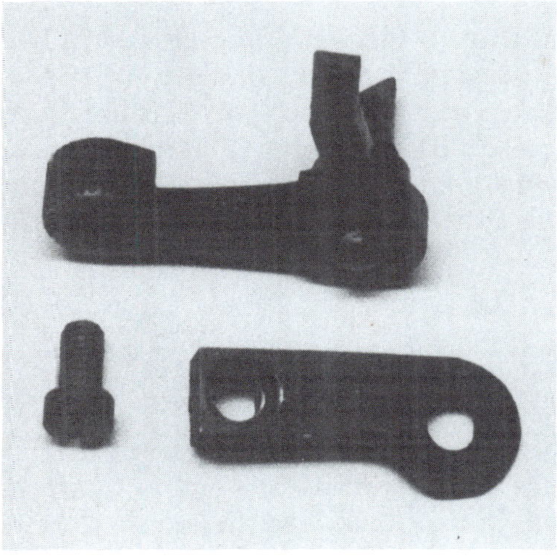

Differences in Fittings

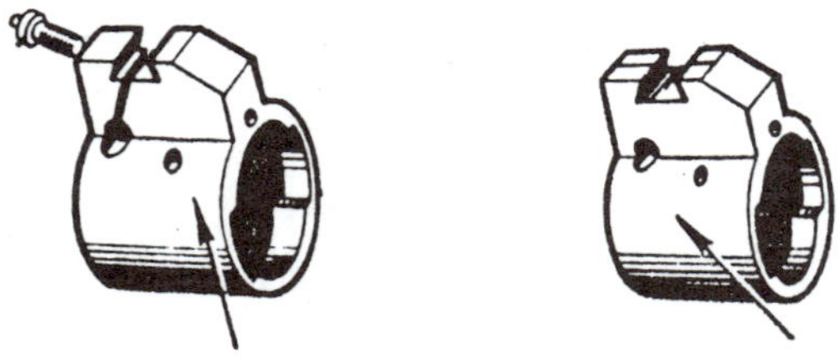

Foresight blocks were initially made in the Mark 1 version of milled steel, left, with a special reverse slot screw, which was tightened to hold the foresight blade. The Mark II version, right, eliminated the reverse slot screw and held the foresight blade by friction only. Both types of blocks were secured to the barrel by a cross pin.

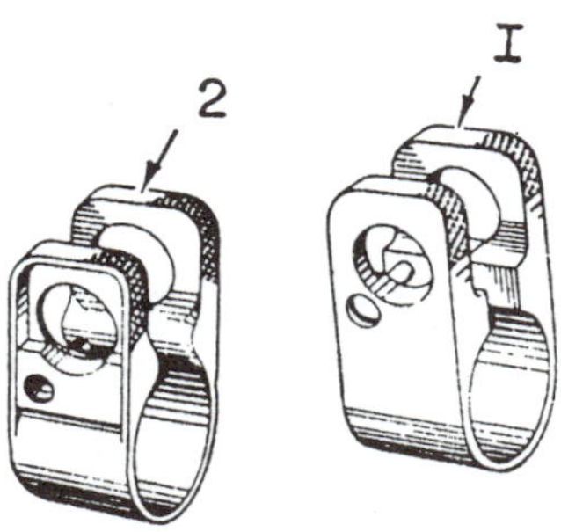

The Mark 1 foresight protector, right, was made of milled steel and appeared on virtually all early Number 4 Mark 1 and Mark 1* rifles. Once production shortcuts became commonplace, the Mark II foresight protector, left, made its appearance, being made from steel stampings. This version often found its way onto Savage and Long Branch manufactured Mark 1* rifles.

The four types of foresight blades made for the Number 4 series of rifles were the Mark 1, Mark 1*, Mark II and Mark III. Differences were in the blade's length and the slot in the base. All types have been found on both Mark 1 and Mark 1* rifles.

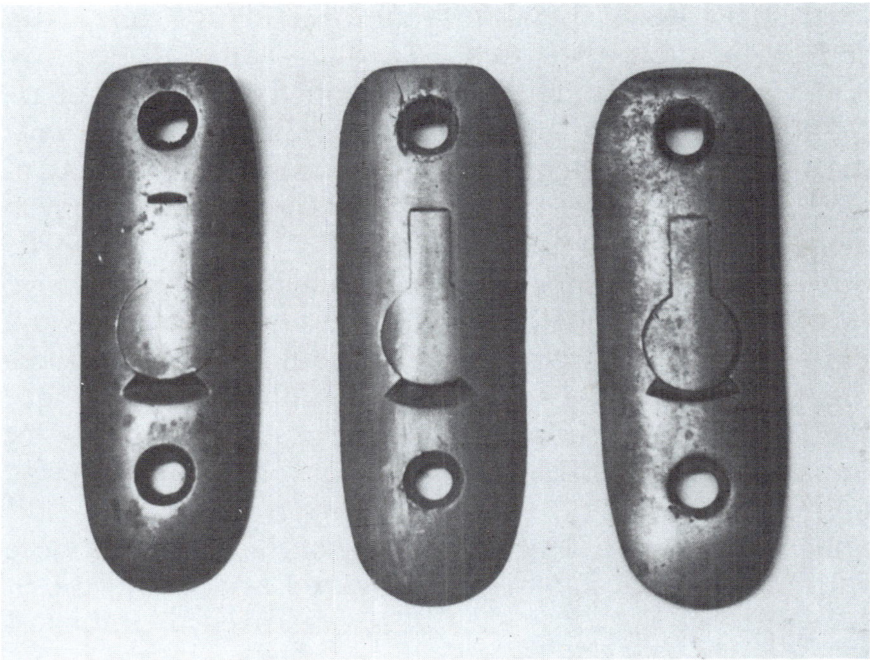

Three types of buttplates were made for Number 4 rifles during their lifetime. From left, brass buttplate found on early Number 4 Mark 1 rifles and many rifles refurbished after the war; gray pot metal buttplate often found on Number 4 Mark 1* rifles made at the Long Branch and Savage manufacturing plants; and a steel buttplate, found on Canadian made Number 4 Mark 1* rifles.

the Number 4 Mark 1 was more complex than was desired at that time, due to the difficulty and cost involved in machining and assembling it. In the Number 4 Mark 1* model, that first rearsight was eliminated in favor of a two-position peep battle sight, designated the Mark 2. This rearsight, sometimes known as the "L-flip" sight, is graduated at 300 and 600 yards, depending which arm is flipped upwards.

While easier to manufacture, the Mark 2 rearsight never had much popularity with the troops, and was soon replaced by the Mark 3 and Mark 4 rearsights, both of which were stamped from sheet steel. They had sliding, lockable apertures, and were graduated to 1,300 yards. While similar to the Mark 1 rearsight, the Mark 3 and Mark 4 versions did not have the robust steadiness and stiffness of the first model. Ultimately, when British armourers put Number 4 rifles through "Factory Thorough Repair" (FTR) after the Second World War, they invariably retrofitted FTR rifles with Mark 1 rearsights.

In another attempt to cut manufacturing time, the Savage Arms Company developed a method of rifling Lee Enfield barrels with only two grooves, instead of the standard five grooves for .303 barrels. The British tested the two groove barrels quite extensively, and could find no appreciable difference in quality or accuracy. Production of two groove barrels was approved in 1941, and many of these barrels were fitted to Canadian and US-manufactured Number 4 Mark 1* rifles.

Factory Codes for the Number 4 Rifle

Identification marks were placed on all British, Canadian and United States manufactured Number 4 rifles. Number 4 rifles were marked, either by stamping or engraving, on the left side of the body and the socket.

Arsenal	*Code*	*Comments*
British		
Maltby	**M**	**• most commonly seen**
	RM	**• rarely seen**
	ROF(M)	**• scarce marking**
Fazakerley	**ROF(F)**	**• very common**
	F	**• very common**
	FY	**• rarely seen**
BSA (Shirley)	**B**	**• scarce marking**
	85B	**• rarely seen**
	M47	**• very common**

[ROF is Royal Ordnance Factory]

Canadian		
Long Branch	**LB**	**• very common**
United States		
Savage	**S**	**• very common**

Number 4 Mark 2

It was well after the end of World War II — 31 March 1949 to be exact — when the British finally upgraded the Number 4 rifle to the Mark 2 model. And in doing so, the major change to the rifle lay in the trigger mechanism.

There was some contemporary criticism of Number 4 Mark 1 and Mark 1* rifles in regard to the trigger letoff. In those two marks, the trigger was pinned to the trigger guard, which then was attached to the receiver by a vertical front guard screw and a horizontal rear guard screw.

A small number of critics charged, that since the trigger was pinned to the guard and not the receiver, it was affected by changes in the wood furniture, such as swelling caused by absorption of water. The British tested these theories, but never issued any conclu-

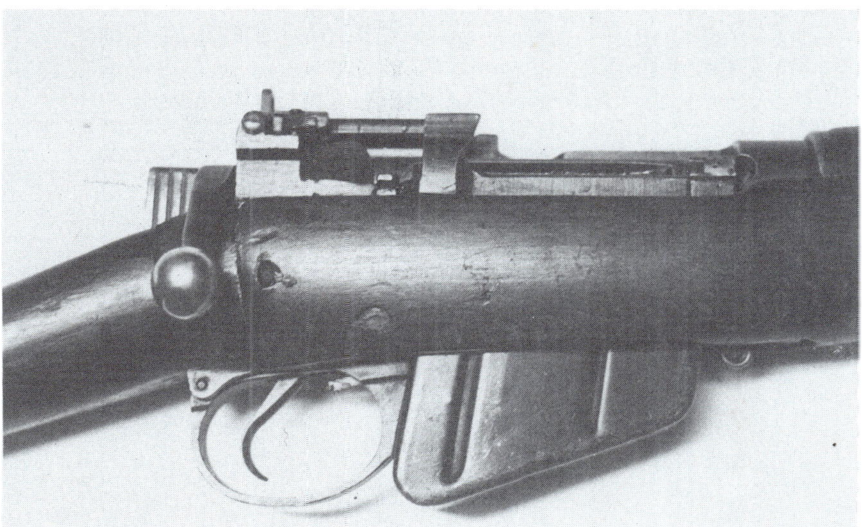

Number 4 Mark 2 rifles can be distinguished by the cross screw at the center rear of the forend. The screw was necessary to secure the wood furniture after it had been altered to fit the Mark 2 trigger.

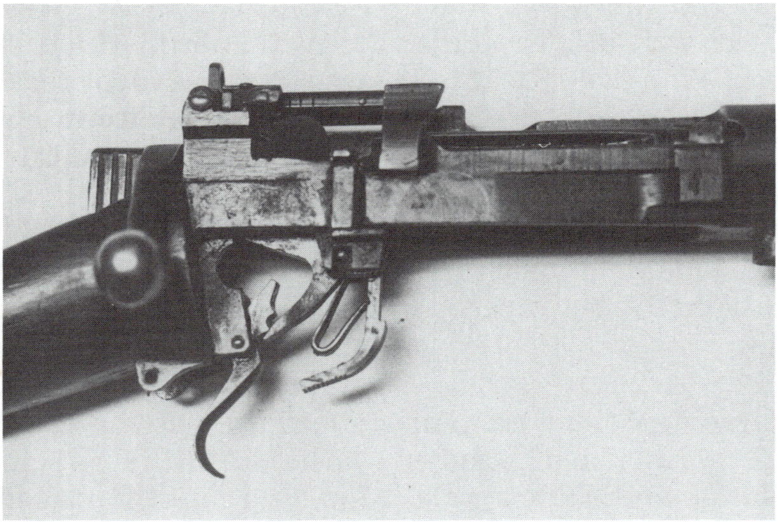

The Mark 2 trigger can be seen in its fixture on the front of the socket. The prior models, the Mark 1 and Mark 1* rifles, had their triggers pinned to the trigger guard. This arrangement led some critics to complain that swelling of the woodwork due to the absorption of moisture caused a binding action on the Mark 1 and Mark 1* triggers. This was judged to be a cause of inaccuracy, and was remedied with the Mark 2 trigger.

sive reports which would verify the charges of the critics. However, in 1949 the British government did introduce the Mark 2 model which had a new design of trigger mechanism.

In this model, the trigger was mounted directly on the receiver, being retained in a fixture brazed to the action. This took the place of having the trigger pinned to the trigger guard. With the trigger now on the receiver, other modifications became necessary. The trigger guard itself was slightly redesigned, and the forend had some additional wood removed from it to accommodate the new trigger fixture.

Lastly, since a considerable piece of wood was

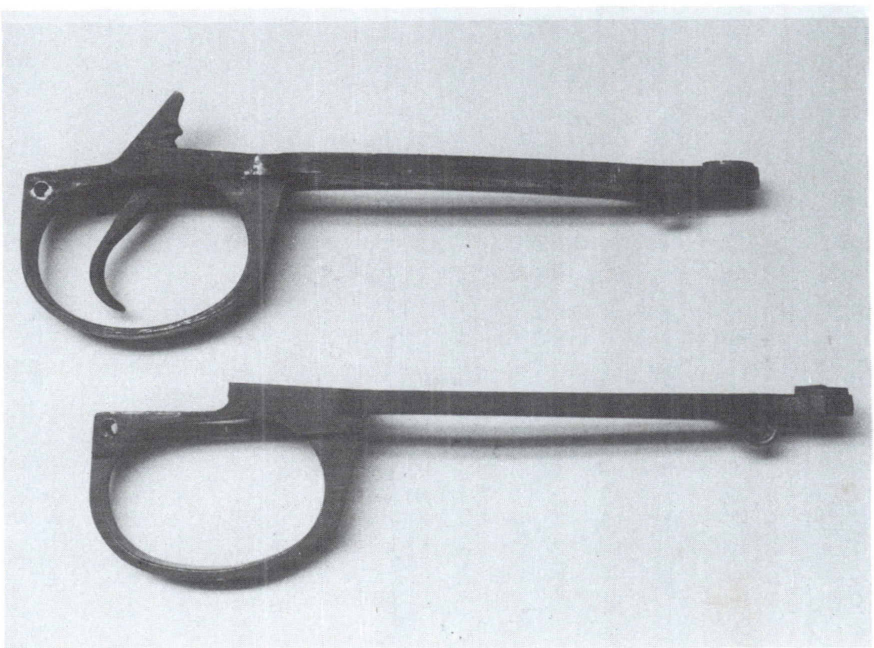

The trigger guard for the Number 4 Mark 2 rifle, bottom, shows the marked contrast in the absence of the trigger and trigger pin from the whole assembly. Many Mark 1 trigger guards were refurbished to the Mark 2 type, while thousands of Mark 2 trigger guards were manufactured anew.

removed from the rear of the forend, a crossbolt was added to provide stability and retain the back portion of the forend.

The critics of the Mark 1 trigger ultimately seem to have been proven correct, since a number of British sources, from the Army itself to target shooting organizations, have shown the Mark 2 trigger to be more reliable than its predecessor. In fact, when the British Army chose an action on which to design its 7.62mm NATO competition target rifle, it chose the Mark 2 action or its converted variants.

Number 4 Mark 1/2

The Number 4 Mark 1/2 was a Mark 1 upgraded to a Mark 2.

This model is essentially a Number 4 Mark 1 rifle, converted to the standards of the Number 4 Mark 2.

The trigger was removed from the trigger guard, and placed into a fixture brazed to the rear of the action. The trigger guard was then modified, as well as the forend, to fit the new fixture.

Most often, the rifle was completely rebuilt, having new furniture installed, as well as new metal fittings. In most cases, a Mark 1 micrometer rearsight was installed.

Once the refurbishment was complete, the rifle was essentially a new one, perhaps only occasionally showing an arsenal repair in the wood furniture.

Rifles converted to Mark 1/2 models were those made by British factories at Fazakerley, BSA (Shirley),

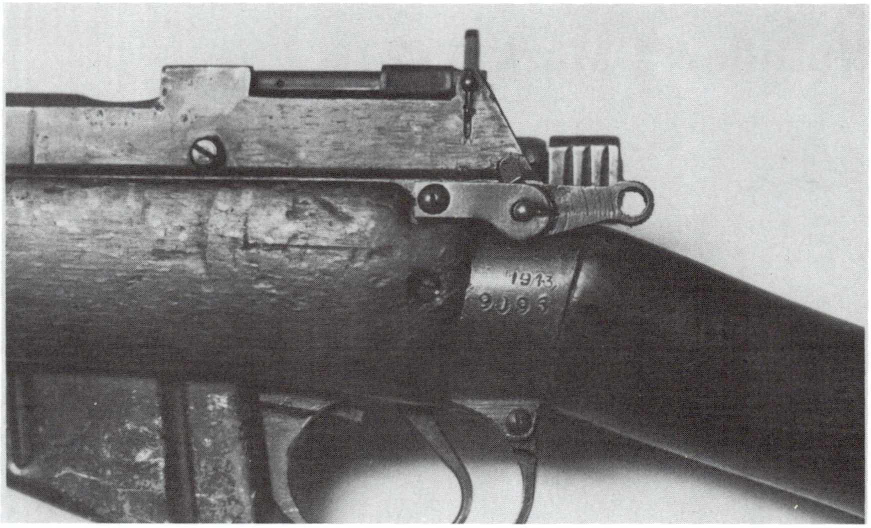

Many refurbished Number 4 Mark 1/2 rifles retain the markings of their original heritage. This Mark 1/2 rifle began its life as a BSA Shirley-manufactured rifle in 1943 (note the "B" stamped above the date on the left socket. The new designation of Number 4 Mark 1/2 ROF(F) /49, engraved on the left side of the action, is barely visible above and to the left of the ejector screw.

and Maltby, as well as early Number 4 Mark 1 rifles made by Savage under contract, prior to Lend-Lease. Rifles were upgraded to Mark 1/2 at the Fazakerley factory.

Number 4 Mark 1/3

This model was a conversion of the Mark 1* designation to the standards of the Number 4 Mark 2. As with the Mark 1/2, the trigger was placed into a fixture brazed to the rear of the action, and the trigger guard and forend modified to fit the new fixture.

Since only two manufacturers made the Mark 1* model, conversions to Mark 1/3 designation are found only on Long Branch and Savage rifles. In most instances, the conversions were carried out at the Fazakerley factory in England.

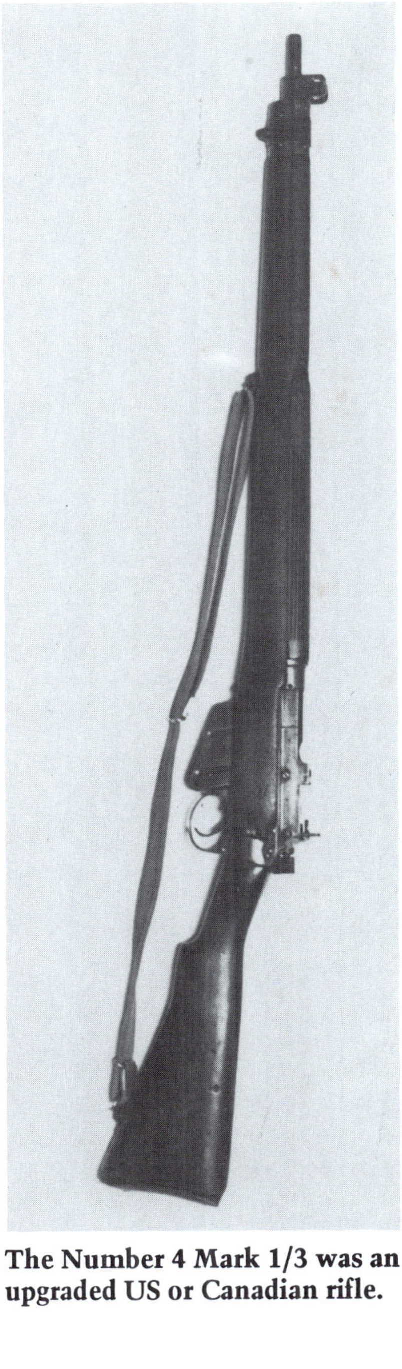

The Number 4 Mark 1/3 was an upgraded US or Canadian rifle.

Number 4 Mark 1 (T)

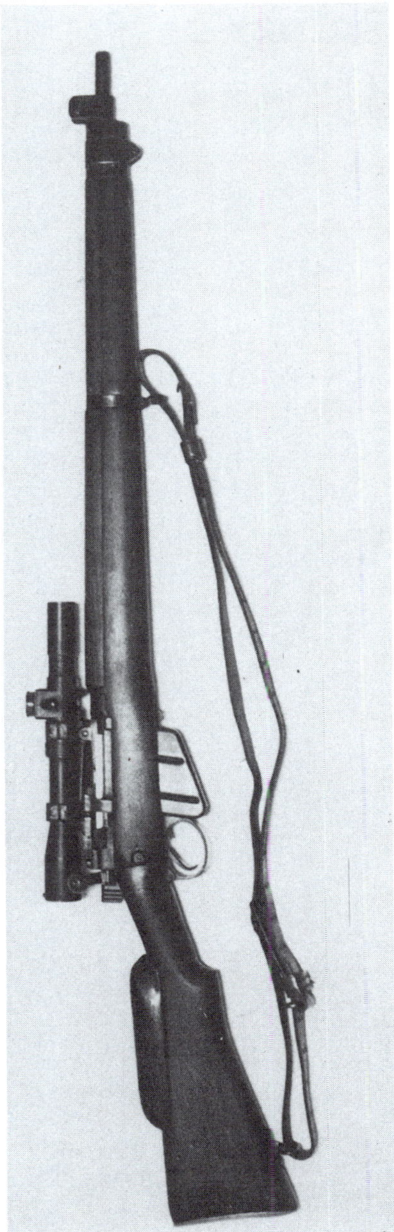

Britian's World War II sniper rifle, the Number 4 Mark 1(T).

By 1942, a new sniper rifle was officially introduced on the British List of Changes, although it had been issued to commandos and special troops a year before. This was the Lee Enfield Rifle Number 4 Mark 1 (T), fitted with the Number 32 Mark 1 telescopic sight.

Basically, it was a specially-accurized Number 4 Mark 1 rifle with base pads fitted to the receiver to take a large, cast mount with thumbscrews for attaching to the weapon. The rifle was fitted with a wooden cheekpiece, screwed to the top of the buttstock, and a revolving swivel in place of the front guard screw.

A two-piece leather sling of US manufacture was usually issued with the sniper rifle as its issue sling.

Conversion of rifles to sniper equipments was usually contracted out to civilian gunmaking firms, and a majority of the Num-

The British Sniper's Equipment

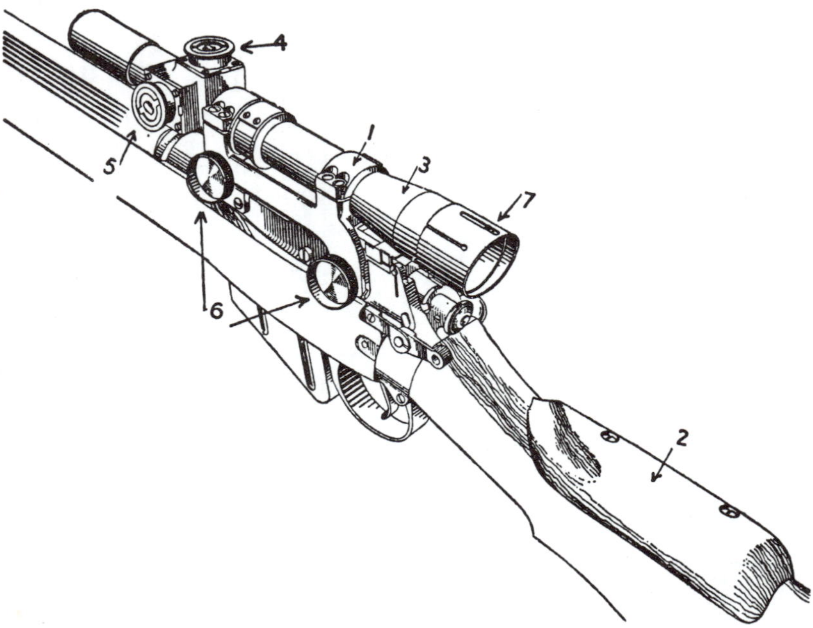

1. Bracket, or Holder
2. Cheek Rest
3. Number 32 Mark 1 telescope
4. Range (elevation) Drum
5. Deflection (windage) Drum
6. Clamping screws

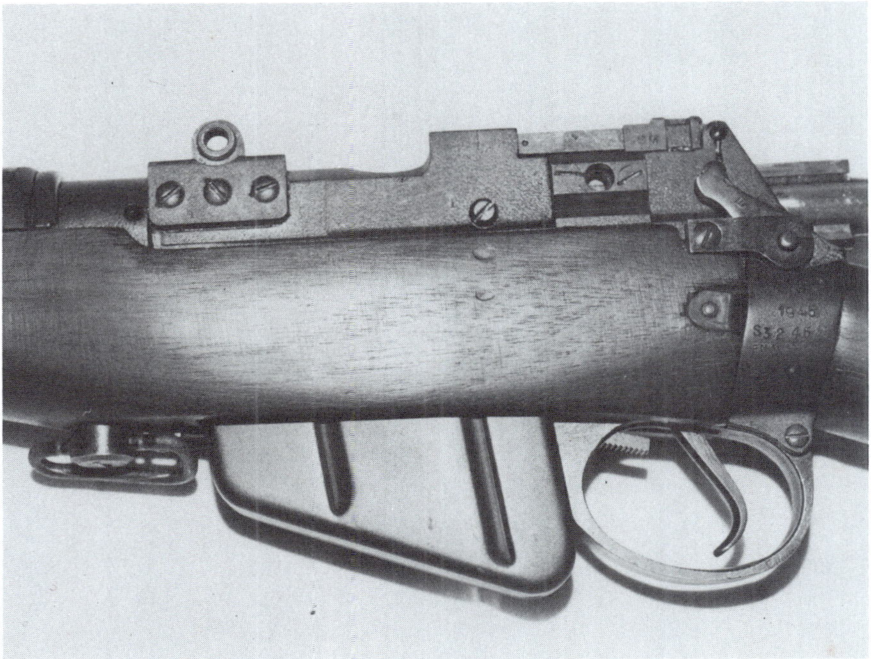

Mounting tabs, also called base pads, were mounted on the left side of the receiver of specially-selected Number 4 rifles. The tabs were screwed and silver soldered to the receiver to prevent them from shifting during use. Also shown is the revolving guard screw swivel at the front of the trigger guard.

ber 4 Mark 1 (T) sniper rifle conversions were set up by the well-known London gunmakers, Holland and Holland. These equipments can be distinguished by the code "S51" stamped on the underside of the buttstock.

Once the sniper equipment was properly mated with its mount, telescopic sight and other components, the complete equipment was given a test for accuracy. This entailed putting seven of seven shots into a five-inch circle at 200 yards. In addition, many rifles also were tested at 400 yards, where they had to put six of seven shots into a ten-inch circle.

Sniper rifles were zeroed for use with both the telescopic sight and the Mark 1 micrometer rearsight.

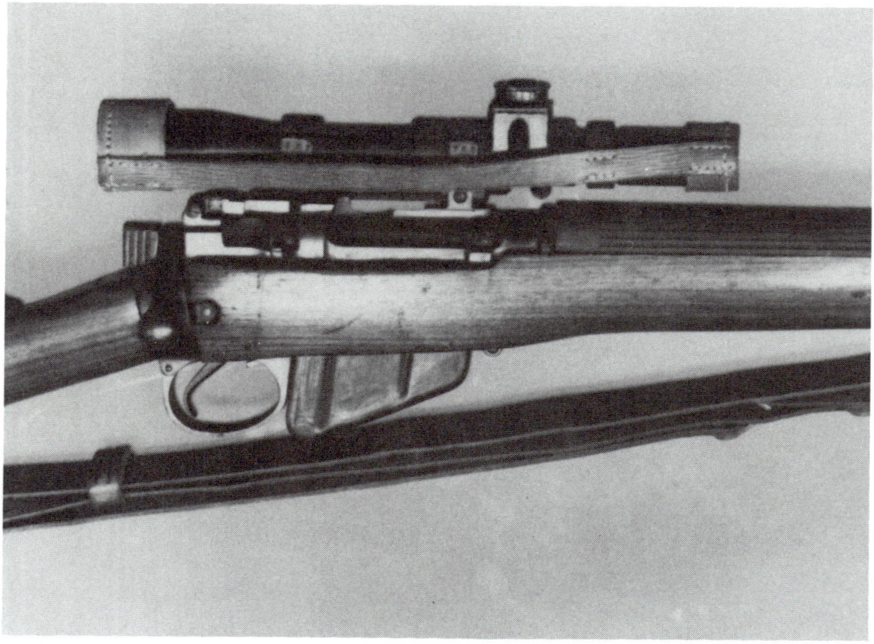

Lens covers made of leather, often featuring an attached keeper, were issued with each Number 4 Mark 1(T) sniper equipment. Pictured is a Number 32 Mark 3 telescopic sight.

The Number 32 Mark 1 telescopic sight was the first of three scope types issued to British snipers during World War II. The Mark 1 was of three-power magnification, with a nine-degree field of view, and had a sliding brass eyeshade, as well as provisions for adjusting elevation and deflection through exterior knobs.

The Number 32 Mark 2 scope was an improved version of first mark, differing mainly in the internal mechanism. The Mark 2 scope was externally the same as the Mark 1, except the eyeshade was omitted.

The Number 32 Mark 3, also of three-power magnification, changed the field of view and the eye relief to 8.5 inches and 2.5 inches respectively. It was waterproofed, where its predecessors were not, and its lenses bloomed to improve light gathering.

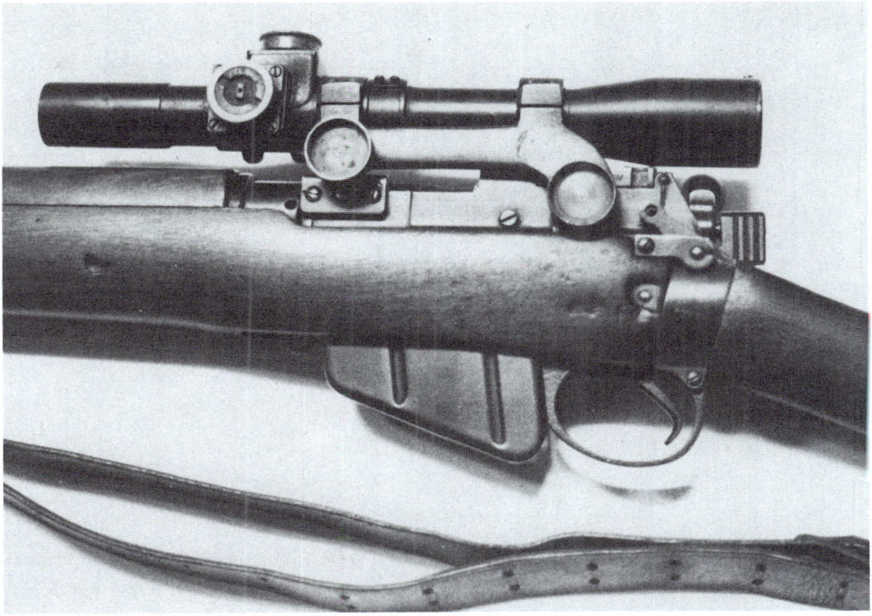

This Number 4 Mark 1(T) is fitted with a Number 32 Mark 2 telescopic sight. The Mark 2 scope was externally very similar to the Mark 1, but did not have the sliding brass eyeshade.

The Number 4 sniping rifle was issued in a wooden chest with leather handles at the balance point, while the scope was enclosed in a metal carrying case to prevent damage when dismounted from the rifle.

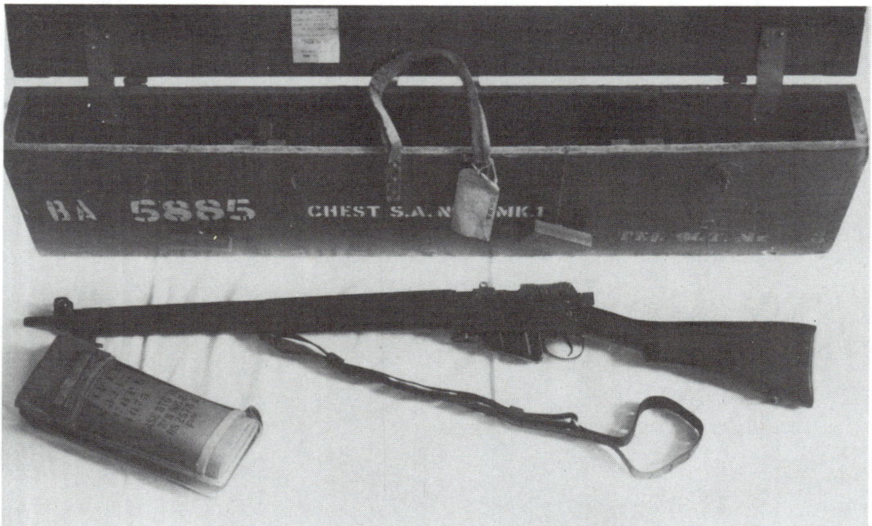

The British sniper was issued his rifle in a wooden chest with leather carrying handles. Inside, in addition to the rifle, scope and mount, was a scope can to hold the scope when dismounted, leather lens covers, adjusting tools for the Mark 1 and Mark 2 scopes, and a lens polishing cloth. The scope can shown is the Number 8 Mark 2 model, canvas covered metal. The Mark 1 model was a rectangular steel box with fixing posts inside to hold the scope securely. Both the scope cans had leather carrying straps.

No.4 Sniper Rifle Instructions

[This material is taken from the booklet, ***Small Arms Training, Rifle, 1942,*** *published by the British War Office.]*

1. General. The No.4 rifle can be fitted with the No.32 telescopic sight for use as a sniper's rifle, in which case it is issued in a chest, S.A. No.15, together with the items listed below, as a complete equipment.

The rifle is fitted with a special sling, a cheek rest, and two pads to take the telescopic sight. In the chest is also packed the telescopic sight in a metal case with a leather carrying strap, complete with bracket, leather protecting caps, an adjusting tool, and a polishing cloth. This cloth must only be used for cleaning the lenses and must be kept clean. Telescopic sights are paired with rifles and are **NOT** interchangeable. The magnification of the telescope is 3.

2. Focusing. It is neither necessary nor possible to alter the focus of the telescopic sight.

3. To attach telescope to rifle. Remove telescope from its box by unscrewing the large-headed clamping screws and attach to the pads on the rifle, partially tightening the rear clamping screw first and finally screwing both fully home.

Sniper Rifle Instructions ... *continued*

4. Adjustment of sight. The telescope is graduated for elevation from 0 to 1,000 yards, and can be adjusted in 50 yard clicks by turning the range drum until the required range is opposite the pointer mark.

Lateral adjustment is also possible by turning the deflection drum on the left of the telescope. This drum is graduated in minutes of angle in two minute clicks up to 16 minutes each side of zero. (A minute of angle equals approximately one inch on the target for every 100 yards of range.)

Example: If, when firing at 300 yards, a shot is observed to strike one foot to the left of the mark, turn the deflection drum anti-clockwise 2 clicks = 4 minutes = 12 inches.

5. Method of aiming.

- Use aiming and head rests.

- Sights upright. Cross wire a good guide when actually aiming.

- Close disengaged eye.

- Eye about 2 to 3 inches away. A full field of view must be obtained. If floating aperture is visible, the eye is either too near or too far away from the telescope.

Sniper Rifle Instructions ... *continued*

• Direct the top of the pointer in the centre of the target. Centering of sight in aperture is automatic.

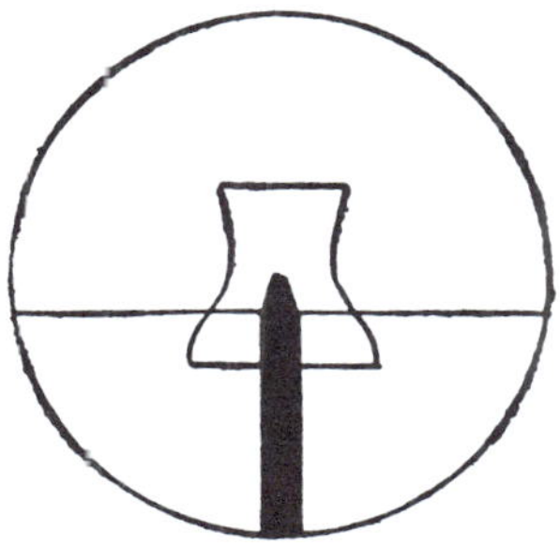

6. Zeroing

General considerations.

• **Examination before test**. The rifle and telescopic sight must be examined by the armourer before test, to ensure that all screws are tight, and that the rifle is stocked up correctly, free from nickeling and oil.

• **Weather conditions.** Good shooting light, and the calmest available weather conditions must be chosen. Sights will be set at 100 yards.

• **Range.** 100 yards from the foresight to the target.

Sniper Rifle Instructions ... *continued*

• **Position**. Lying. Forearm and wrist rested (not the rifle).

• **Targets.** Any suitable target with a two-inch black aiming mark. A vertical line is to be drawn through the centre of the mark.

• **Point of aim**. Lowest central point of the aiming mark.

• **Method.** Two shots will be fired into the bank to warm the barrel. A group of five rounds will be fired. The necessary standard of grouping is 3 inches at 100 yards.

• After any adjustment has been made, the rifle should be re-tested and corrected as necessary, as the figures given are approximations, but if used as a guide, will save time and ammunition. **Note**: No vertical or lateral error should ever be left on a sniper's rifle.

To adjust for errors

• First alter setting of range and/or deflection drums so as to bring the MPI (mean point of impact) to coincide with the point of aim. *Note:* If the shots are striking to the left of the point of aim, turn the deflection drum anti-clockwise; if to the right, turn the drum clockwise.

Sniper Rifle Instructions ... *continued*

• **Elevation** is adjusted by placing the adjusting tool over the range drum so that the slot on the end of the upper tommy bar and the projections on the base of the lower tommy bar engage with the projection on the central pin and in the slots in the clamp ring respectively.

Loosen the clamp ring by turning the lower tommy bar one-half turn anti-clockwise, at the same time holding both the upper tommy bar and the range drum stationary.

Still holding the upper tommy bar stationary, rotate the range drum until the range to the target is shown opposite the point mark.

Holding the upper tommy bar and the range drums stationary, tighten the clamp ring by turning the lower tommy bar in a clockwise direction. An assistant to hold the range drum will facilitate adjustments.

• **Deflection** errors are eliminated by following the above procedure with the deflection drum, moving the drum until the figure 0 is opposite the pointer mark.

Sniper Sling Instructions

[This material is taken from the booklet, ***Small Arms Training, Rifle, 1942,*** *published by the British War Office.]*

General description.

The sling consists briefly of two parts (A and B as shown in Figure 1). Part A is longer than Part B and is attached to the upper sling swivel and forms the principal part. Part B is much shorter, is fixed to the lower sling swivel and is connected with A by a metal link, so enabling the rifle to be slung.

The object of the sling.

- To assist shooting by keeping the rifle steady, when cover is not available.
- To enable the rifle to be carried on the shoulder in the normal manner.

How to fit to rifle.

Take the larger Part A, which forms the upper part and do as follows:

- Slide the sling keeper (leather band) down to within about 9 inches from the sling hooks, place the plain end through the link

Sniper Sling Instructions ... *continued*

attached to Part B till it touches the keeper, bend the sling round and slide it once more back through the keeper, thus forming a leather loop for the metal link attached to B.

• Slip the second keeper over the plain end of the sling and place this end through the upper sling swivel, double over and bring back through the second keeper and engage first pair of holes with the hooks.

• Place Part B through the lower sling swivel, and engage hooks with holes so that sling hangs sufficiently loose to enable rifle to be carried slung on the shoulder.

How to use the sling.

• Loosen the lower loop of the sling so that it hangs free as shown in Figure 2.

• Insert the left arm through the upper loop from right to left. (To facilitate doing this, the sling should be given a half turn in an anti-clockwise direction.) Hoist the upper loop well up the arm so that it is near the shoulder and well above the biceps muscle (see Figure 3).

• Pull the keeper (Figure 4) close against the arm to keep the upper loop in place.

Sniper Sling Instructions ... *continued*

• Move the left hand over the top of the sling and grasp the rifle near the top sling swivel so as to cause the sling to lie smoothly along the back of the hand and wrist.

• The lower loop, not used in shooting, should be so loose as to prevent any pull upon it.

• Neither end of the sling will be removed from either swivel.

Having carried out the above and assumed the lying position, when in the aim the sling should be just sufficiently tight to offer support, but not so tight as to have a tendency to pull the left elbow to the left or to prevent proper circulation of the blood in the upper portion of the left arm.

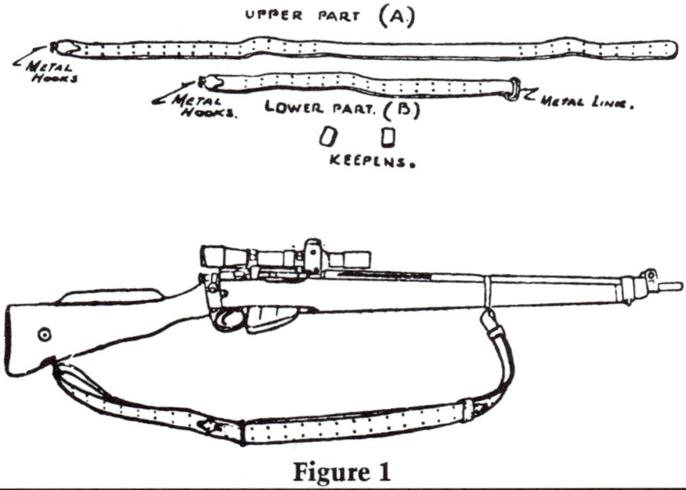

Figure 1

Sniper Sling Instructions ... *continued*

Figure 2

Sniper Sling Instructions ... *continued*

Figure 3

Sniper Sling Instructions ... *continued*

Figure 4

Bayonets for the Number 4 Rifle

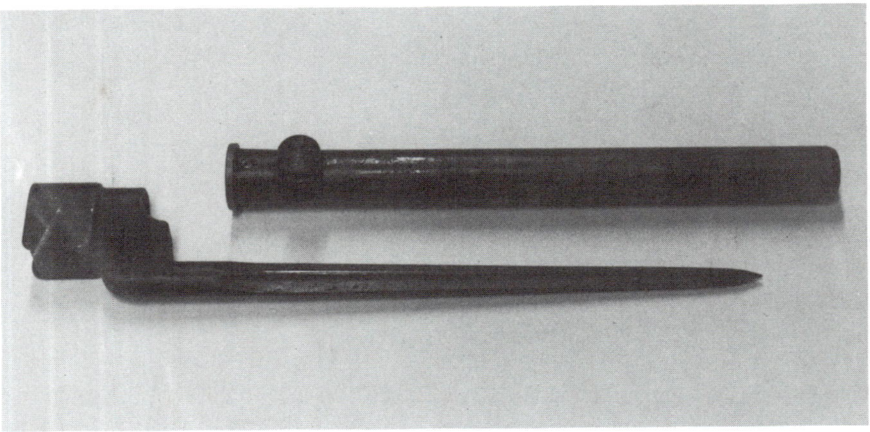

The first bayonet approved for use with the Number 4 Mark 1 rifle was the Mark 1 model, commonly known as the cruciform bayonet, due to the cross section of its blade. In fact, it was quite difficult to refer to the Mark 1's blade as such, since it was more of a spike-like poker than a traditional blade. In any event, when fixed, it was found that bayonet fighting with the new model on the Number 4 rifle was appreciably easier than with the old SMLE Number 1 rifle and the Pattern 1907 blade bayonet. But ultimately, the need for more and more production was the death knell of the Mark 1 cruicform bayonet, since its blade was so difficult to fabricate. The Mark 1 is shown with its paralle-sided steel scabbard.

The Mark II Bayonet Arrives

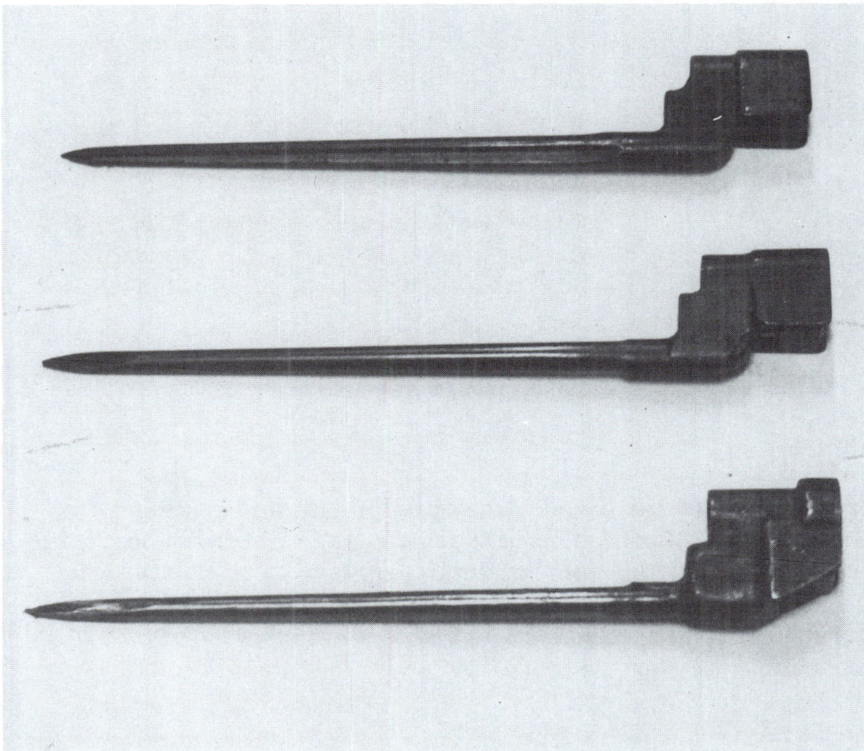

Three types of bayonet for the Number 4 rifle are shown here. From top, the Mark 1, Mark II, and Mark III. The chief difference between the Mark 1 and the other two is in the construction of the blade. The Mark II and III featured a smooth spike, which was considerably easier to manufacture than the cruciform pattern of the Mark 1. Note the crude casting of the Mark III's socket.

A Post-war Blade

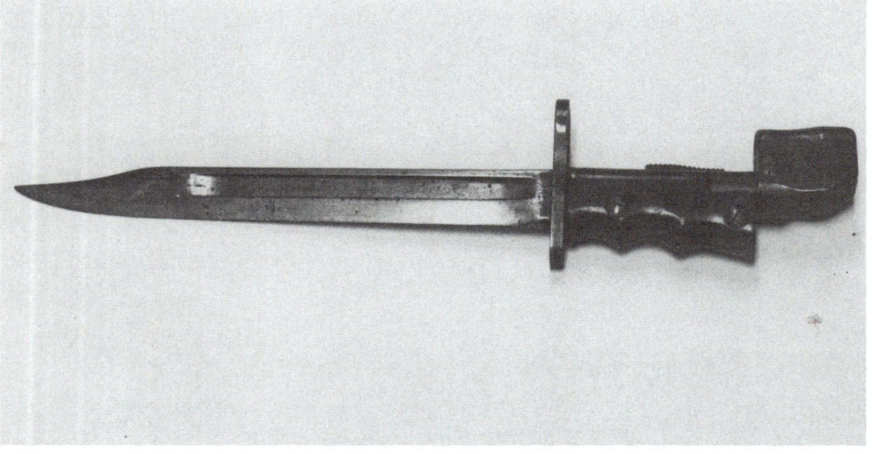

A blade bayonet finally was developed for use on the Number 4 rifle, the Number 7 Mark 1. This bayonet was first intended to be fixed to the Sten submachine gun, but developers gave up on that idea and decided to attach it to the Number 4. The Number 7 Mark 1, developed after the end of World War II, featured an eight inch blade and composite grips.

A Second Blade Bayonet

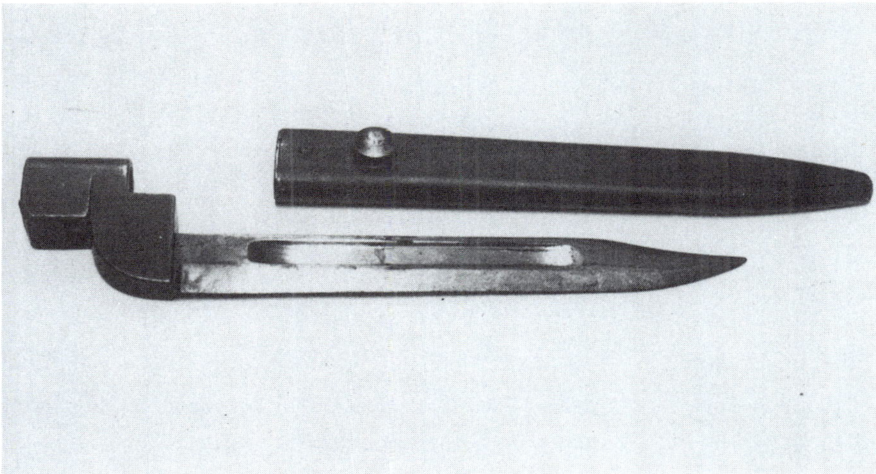

Another blade bayonet for the Number 4 rifle appeared after the war, the Number 9 Mark 1. This model appears to have taken a step backwards, since the grip has disappeared (see Number 7 bayonet) and been replaced by the earlier style socket only. The Number 9 had a blade just under eight inches in length. This model is pictured with its scabbard, which was common to the Number 7, the Number 9 and the Number 5 (jungle carbine) bayonets.

Excalibur Publications
PO Box 36
Latham, NY 12110-0036